Finding Nana

Wendy Christoffel

Copyright © 2023 Wendy Christoffel
All rights reserved
First Edition

PAGE PUBLISHING
Conneaut Lake, PA

First originally published by Page Publishing 2023

ISBN 978-1-6624-7411-8 (hc)
ISBN 978-1-6624-7412-5 (digital)

Printed in the United States of America

For my heartlights Torin, Drew, Jessica and Sherril

Bergen County Animal Shelter, Ramapo-Bergen Animal Refuge and St. Hubert's Animal Welfare Center will share in a portion of the profits from the sale of this book.

This is a true story written for children and others who love animals…especially dogs.

On a cold, rainy morning in early October, Alice was driving to work.

Since there was a traffic jam on the road ahead, Alice decided to drive down a side street so she would not be late. It was not a nice street. It ran along the railroad tracks and there were large holes in the road. Alice drove very carefully so her wheels would not go into the holes.

Just as she was coming to the end of the street, a dog appeared. Its hair was dark and shaggy and its long tail hung down into the puddles. It was walking along the railroad tracks that ran right through the middle of this gloomy part of town. There were no houses here, just old, boarded up factories, so Alice wondered where the dog might be going.

Alice opened the car window and called to the dog, "Are you all right?"

The dog turned its head and looked at Alice. It appeared to be very dirty. Alice thought it might also be hungry. She got out of the car and knelt down.

"Are you hungry?" called Alice.

"Do you want this?" she asked, as she held out the baloney sandwich she had packed for lunch.

The dog crossed the road and ate Alice's sandwich.

Then the shaggy dog wagged its tail and rubbed its wet face on the sleeve of Alice's bright yellow jacket.

"Oh, dear," said Alice, "you've made my jacket awfully dirty."

The dog lowered its head as if it thought Alice had scolded it. Alice held the dog's head in her hands and lifted its face up to hers. She brushed aside the hair that was hiding the dog's gentle, brown eyes. Then, as they looked into each other's eyes, Alice saw how thankful the dog was for the food.

"That's all right," said Alice. "You're just thanking me, aren't you?"

She knew that was just what the dog was doing because, once again, it wagged its tail.

As Alice was petting the dog, she felt its neck for a collar. There was none. Just as she thought, the dog was a stray and had not been cared for in a very long time. Not only did it need a bath, but its hair was so badly matted that it hung in clumps all over its body.

"You don't belong here," said Alice, as she wiped a tear from her eye. And then, she began to think…

The house that Alice, her husband Matthew and their young son Drew lived in was rather small. They also shared it with two cats named Fanny and Fluff and a golden retriever, Nellie. But Alice decided that once Matthew had seen this gentle, loving dog, he would agree there was room for just one more pet.

And so, feeling that everything would work out just fine, Alice opened the car door and offered the dog, that she now noticed was a female, a ride in her car. But the dog just backed away.

"Perhaps," said Alice, "if I drive very slowly, you'll follow me to work."

And that is just what happened.

As Alice parked her car in front of the building, the dog appeared at the corner. She followed, as Alice headed for the front door with a red plaid blanket over her arm. She spread the blanket on the top step, out of the rain, and her new friend stayed there all day, curled up and sleeping.

At the end of the day, Alice went to check on the dog. But all she found was the red plaid blanket. Disappointed, she folded up the blanket and started for home. To her surprise, there was the dog, sitting right next to Alice's car!

"Do you want to come home with me?" asked Alice. The dog barked, turned in circles and wagged her tail.

Alice laughed, patted the dog's head and spread the blanket over the back seat of the car. The dog jumped in, rubbed her face into the blanket and settled in for the ride home.

When Alice returned home, she hid the dog behind her and rang the doorbell. Matthew opened the door.

"Did you forget your key?" he asked.

"No, Dear," replied Alice, as she stepped away from the dog. "I asked her if she wanted to come home with me and she said yes!"

With that, the dog looked up at Matthew and lifted her paw.

"Look, Matt! She likes you!"

"But we already have two cats and a dog," pleaded her husband.

"Please, Matt, just look at those beautiful eyes!"

And that was all it took. They would find room for *one* more pet.

The next morning, Alice called the local animal control officer to let him know she had found a stray. She described the dog and told him just where she had found her. He thanked Alice for calling and said he would let her know if anyone called to claim the stray. No one did.

A visit to the veterinarian Dr. Spicer was next. He examined the dog and told Alice that, aside from needing a good bath, the dog was just fine.

So back home they went and Alice spent the rest of that Saturday morning clipping away the dog's matted hair and giving her a warm, bubbly bath. The dog then sat patiently as Alice dried her with a big, fluffy towel. Then Alice brushed and combed and brushed and combed until, at last, the dog was beautiful! No more dirt or clumps of matted hair! The light tan and soft gray colors in her pretty coat now showed brightly against her dark brown eyes.

Tired from the bath and just content to be well fed and warm, the dog curled up on the red plaid blanket and slept for the rest of the day. The other animals stared at her but seemed to accept the new arrival and did not disturb her sleep. Alice, tired from all the brushing and combing, also took a nap.

That evening, the family had some fun choosing a name for their new dog.

"How about Daisy?" asked Alice. There was silence.

"What about Peppermint Patty?" asked Drew. They all burst into laughter.

"How about Lucy?" asked Alice. They all agreed, that name did not fit at all.

So Alice just sat quietly and thought about the dog's gentle, loving nature. And that is when the name came to her. "Nana!" exclaimed Alice. "She's gentle and loving, just like a nana!" Everyone laughed, and when Alice called "Nana," the dog went to her and wagged its tail and Alice said, "Good girl, Nana!"

Nana was quickly accepted into the household, but Alice soon realized that Nana had not been trained to live in a house. Alice patiently reminded her just what the word *out* meant and that chewing on the rugs was definitely not acceptable behavior. Nana learned quickly and always seemed eager to please Alice.

As the weeks passed, Nana gained more and more weight. Alice thought this was because Nana had a good appetite and always finished all the food that was placed in her bowl.

Then one day, Drew went to his mother and asked, "Is Nana going to have puppies? She looks really round," he said with a giggle.

Alice told her son she did not think so, but did agree that Nana was getting a bit round.

"Time for another visit to Dr. Spicer," said Alice. "He'll probably say she's just a bit overweight."

Alice gave Nana a hug and said, "Let's go find out what the good doctor has to say." Then off they went to Dr. Spicer's friendly office in the quaint, red house on the hill.

"No," Dr. Spicer told Alice. "She's not overweight. She's going to have puppies…four or five, I think." Then he reached into the big, glass jar on his desk and pulled out a tiny, bone-shaped dog biscuit. Nana barked, turned in a circle and wagged her tail. "You're welcome, Nana," he said, laughing.

"Well," sighed Alice, "finding homes for four or five puppies doesn't seem too difficult." She thanked the doctor and hurried home with Nana to share the exciting news.

Soon Alice began preparing for the new arrivals. First, she and Drew brought home books from the library. One described how to make a special box in which the puppies would be born and another explained how to help the mother dog with the births. They found it all very interesting.

Then Alice knitted Nana a cozy dog sweater using wool yarn the color of ripe strawberries. Cold weather was on the way, so Alice wanted to be sure that Nana would be warm and toasty when she went outside.

One evening in late November, Nana, now very, very large, waddled into Alice's bedroom and began turning in circles and scratching the carpet. When Alice looked down she saw the first of Nana's puppies and, ever so gently, picked it up. It was soft and warm and fit in the palm of Alice's hand. She placed it in the box that was in a warm corner of the room. Nana hopped in and licked the puppy all over. Then she settled down to deliver the rest of her puppies.

Soon the other puppies began arriving and as puppy number 4 was being born, Alice noticed there was a puppy missing. She and Matthew searched until they found it hidden under Nana's back leg. But it was not breathing!

Just then, Drew came into the room. Seeing the limp puppy in Alice's hand, he yelled, "Mom, do something!"

They all took turns rubbing the puppy's chest and Matthew blew air into its tiny mouth. It began to wiggle…it was alive! They gave the puppy back to Nana and she licked its face and, using her nose, gently nudged it in with the other puppies.

After puppy number 5 was born, everyone thought that was the last of the litter. But then Nana delivered another…and another… and another, until there were eight puppies.

Everyone thought *that* was the end of it. But then Nana gave birth to puppy number 9. Thinking she was surely finished, Alice, Matthew and Drew left Nana with her puppies and went to bed.

In the morning, Alice counted the puppies just to make sure they were all safe. To her surprise, there were now ten puppies—nine females and one male. They were all lined up in rows, having their breakfast. Nana had given birth to her tenth puppy after the family had gone to bed.

Nana turned out to be a super mom. She cleaned her puppies, nursed them often and watched carefully whenever the curious cats came near, or when Nellie poked her head in to see what all the squeals were about. And if a pup wandered out of the box, Nana would grab it gently by the back of its neck and return it to its bed.

Alice knew the local animal shelter helped in finding homes for animals, so she called to let them know she had ten puppies that would be needing homes. The woman who answered told Alice it would be best if the puppies stayed with their mother until they were at least eight weeks old and then they could be adopted by families on the shelter's list.

Alice breathed a sigh of relief, knowing the shelter would help her to find homes for Nana's ten precious pups.

It was during the next few weeks that the pups began to eat moist puppy food. This was placed in a large metal bowl with a post in the middle so the puppies would not walk through their food.

The puppies were fed a few times a day and soon they were getting quite big. Matthew had built a large indoor pen in which to keep them, but it was getting a bit crowded.

Soon, Alice's phone began ringing with callers asking about Nana's adorable puppies. And since no puppy was to leave before it was eight weeks old, those who called waited patiently for the time when they could take a puppy home.

Mothers and fathers and children with smiling faces soon began arriving at the little house. One by one, a warm, cuddly pup was lovingly wrapped in a blanket, quilt, or old sweater and bundled off to its new home. It was not long before there were just two adorable puppies playing in the large pen.

It was early February and snowing heavily when the last family arrived to choose its puppy. The children could not have been happier! They hugged and stroked their pup as it wagged its tail and licked their faces with its tiny, pink tongue.

Alice watched with delight and Nana barked excitedly as the happy family wrapped its newest member in a soft, pink blanket and hurried into their car for the trip home.

"So much happiness, Nana, you have given *so* much happiness," said Alice, as she patted Nana's head and closed the door against the snowy afternoon.

Now there was just one adorable puppy that had not been adopted. But instead of giving it to a shelter, Alice and Matthew decided the puppy would stay. The family named her Tinky, and there were now two cats, two dogs and one little puppy living in their small house.

As the months went by, the puppy grew bigger and bigger. It would not be long before the family's three large dogs would be crowded into a space too small for them. Also, Alice worked all day, so she was finding it harder and harder to give all the dogs the time they deserved. She needed help, but the rest of the family was just as busy as Alice.

Then one Sunday afternoon in May came an unexpected phone call. It was from a man who asked Alice if she had a dog available for adoption. The animal shelter had given him her name.

"Oh," said Alice, "I wasn't expecting any more calls for a puppy."

The man said he was not interested in a puppy, but an older dog. He explained it was for his elderly parents whose dog had died of old age the year before. He said a puppy would be too much work for them, so they wanted an older dog that was gentle and loving. He was describing Nana!

Alice's heart sank. Nana. They had come so far together. But Alice knew she did not have the time or the room for three dogs.

She felt in her heart that it was unfair to all of them, but especially to Nana, who always looked for extra love and attention.

Alice closed her eyes and took a deep breath before she answered.

"Yes," she said. "You can come this afternoon."

Alice hung up the phone as she wiped a tear from her eye.

The doorbell rang and the dogs barked their greetings from the yard. The man who called came in, followed by his parents, Mr. and Mrs. Mills. They were *so* excited and could not wait to meet Nana.

Alice called Nana in from the yard where she was playing with Nellie and Tinky. Nana greeted the visitors with happy barks and a wagging tail.

Mrs. Mills smiled, patted Nana's head and said, "She's a very nice dog, isn't she?"

"Yes," replied Alice. "She's a *very* nice dog."

Mr. Mills spoke gently to Nana and she listened. She seemed to like him.

"She's just what we're looking for, Dear," he said to his wife. "Shall we take her home and see how she likes us?"

Alice reached for Nana's red leash that hung on a hook behind the kitchen door.

"Here, Nana," called Alice.

Nana went to Alice and as she reached for Nana's collar, Alice whispered into Nana's ear, "I love you, Nana," and put her arms around Nana's neck and hugged her. And it was just like that first time beside the railroad tracks on that cold, rainy day, when they looked into each other's eyes and into each other's heart and began their long and loving journey.

Alice handed Nana's leash to Mr. Mills and gave Nana another hug. Then Nana followed her new family into their car and they all waved goodbye as the car headed down the road.

Alice, Matthew and Drew were all sad that Nana was leaving, but happy that she was going to a loving home. Mr. and Mrs. Mills would have plenty of time to give Nana all the extra love and attention she needed.

Mr. Mills called a few days later to say that Nana had settled in nicely. He told Alice that he took Nana for a walk a few times a day and every day he brushed her beautiful coat. He also told Alice that Mrs. Mills was very impressed with how well behaved Nana was and how much she enjoyed her company. Mr. Mills said it felt good to have a gentle, loving dog sharing their happy home.

The months passed and soon it was October again. The cold winds of autumn were blowing, so Alice searched through the wool clothing she had put away in the spring. There she found Nana's strawberry red sweater. She wrapped it up and sent it to Nana at her new address.

A few days later, Alice received a thank you phone call from Mr. Mills. He laughed as he told Alice how Nana had barked and turned in circles when he opened the unexpected package. Alice smiled as she imagined Nana sniffing the sweater and remembering the one who had made it for her.

That spring, Alice received another phone call from Mr. Mills, asking if she would like to see Nana. Alice was delighted! The day arrived and Mr. Mills brought Nana, on her red leash, to Alice's front door. Alice hugged Nana and told her how happy she was to see her. Mr. Mills had just taken her to be groomed and she looked especially pretty. She was even wearing a bright yellow bow in her hair.

"How are you, Nana, my sweet girl?" asked Alice.

Nana barked, turned in circles and wagged her tail.

Then, as Fanny and Fluff watched from behind a tree, Nana, Tinky and Nellie played together on the front lawn. It was just like old times. But soon it was time for Nana to go home.

Once again, Alice hugged her old friend.

"Goodbye, dear Nana," said Alice.

But this time, Alice was not sad, for she knew that Nana had found a home where she was needed and wanted and where she would be given all the love that one dog's heart could ever hold… and Alice had helped her to find it.

Postscript

When finding Nana along the railroad tracks on that cold, rainy morning, Alice could not have imagined all the happiness Nana and her puppies would bring to so many children, and to Mr. and Mrs. Mills, whose hearts would become filled with love for their precious Nana.

And…you will be happy to know that Nana is still barking, turning in circles and wagging her tail, especially when Mrs. Mills offers her a biscuit or when Mr. Mills holds out her red leash and calls, "Come on, Nana! Let's go for a walk!"

Acknowledgments

How fortunate I was to grow up in a loving and creative home. As I watched my mother Hazel crocheting or playing the piano and my father Ben drawing or writing poetry, my creative spirit was nourished, as was my sense of nurturing when my caring mother tended to a sparrow with an injured wing, then set it free. And I was over the moon when my father brought home a stray dog that followed him home from work one summer night. I named him Pal. He was my first pet.

From an early age, my nine siblings Warren, Frank, Dolores, Diane, Edwin, Marilyn, Dawn, Sherril and Wayne and I were shown how to lovingly care for animals. This was reflected beautifully in the love and care I saw my eldest brother Warren give to the many animals that shared his life. Today, my kind-hearted brother Wayne and his compassionate wife Julie and daughter Britt pay it forward and provide food, shelter and affection to stray cats.

I will be forever grateful to my dearest friend, my sister Sherril. I would recite my poetry to her as we lay in our beds at night. In the darkness, she listened and encouraged me with "Write it down, Wendy." Years later, the manuscript of this book was one of the last pieces I shared with Sherril before she passed on. My beloved sister would be thrilled to know that Finding Nana has become a reality.

My sister Marilyn always looked out for me. She braided my hair in the morning, walked with me to get my first eyeglasses, held my hand at the dentist and stood beside me on my wedding day. She loved the poems I wrote for her, especially the whimsical ones. They were my way of giving back the love she had given me over all those years.

My eternal gratitude to my brother Frank for his courage and his profound inspiration.

My sons Torin and Drew and my granddaughter Jessica shared not only in the lives of the dogs and cats we so loved, but also in the lives of the wild things we fostered in our home. While tending to Gloriana the robin, Scarlet the cardinal, Blueberry the blue jay, Rocky the flying squirrel, Choo Choo and Timmy the gray squirrels, a spunky little chipmunk, a nest of young woodpeckers and a fluffle of bunnies, we embraced a love of

God's creatures. Some of them would become characters in my stories.

Thank you to my loved ones Dee and Dick Sarta, Sharlene and Don Miller Pizza, Nancy Simoneau, Nelda Brickner and Lauren Brickner McDonald for inspiring me. And much gratitude to my dear friend and editor Anthony LaBarbera for his guidance, patience and love.

Dick VanTieghem was a gifted designer and award-winning watercolor artist who assisted me in constructing the book and sketched its preliminary illustrations. He offered to help me when I had no idea of how to put a book together. Dick's generous heart and caring nature made me believe I could do it.

Our dear neighbor Brian Mulroy always had treats and love for my beloved golden retrievers Puma and Cody. I will miss them forever, but Brian assured me that I would one day see them again. Thank you for that comforting thought, Bri.

Bob Tobey's compassion and love has for many years brought comfort to the lives of shelter animals. God bless you, Bob, and all volunteers who give of their time to help animals in need.

If not for the efforts of animal rescuers everywhere, so many precious dogs and cats would go uncared for, perhaps never to know a word of praise, a hug, or a gentle pat on the head. Thank you to all the selfless animal rescuers who save lives every day and who make this a better world.

Lastly and most importantly, a hug for Nana. If not for this gentle, loving sheepdog mix there would be no Finding Nana. She crossed my path, touched my heart and gave me the story that has become this heartfelt children's book.

About the Author

Wendy Christoffel expresses her love of nature through her writings and her art. She lives in Ridgewood, New Jersey with her beautiful, rescued calico cat Ash.

Printed in the USA
CPSIA information can be obtained
at www.ICGtesting.com
LVHW061106091023
760451LV00016B/34